T5-ARZ-555

A Whale of a Tale

by Spencer Brinker

Consultant:
Beth Gambro
Reading Specialist
Yorkville, Illinois

Contents

BEARPORT PUBLISHING

New York, New York

A Whale of a Tale

This is Marco, a cute baby **whale**.

His smile is bright,
and his color
is **pale**.

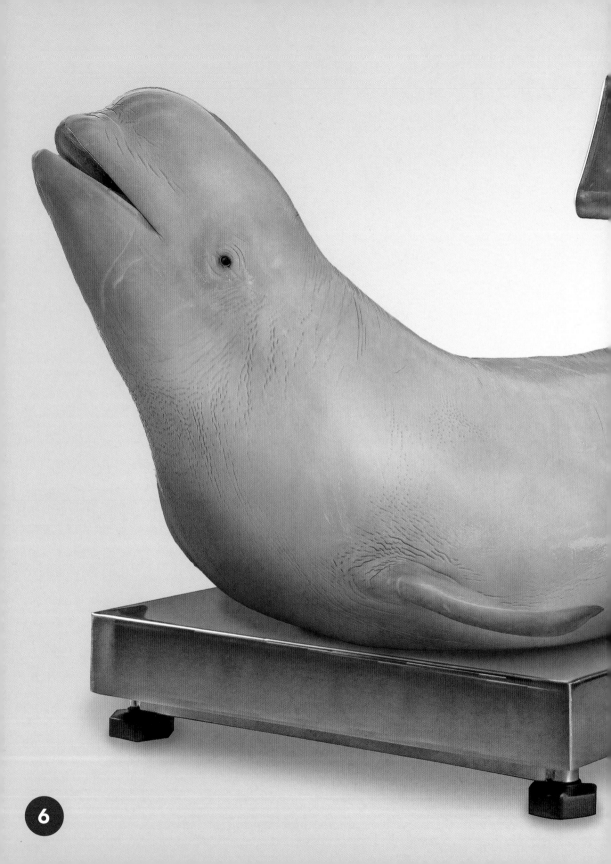

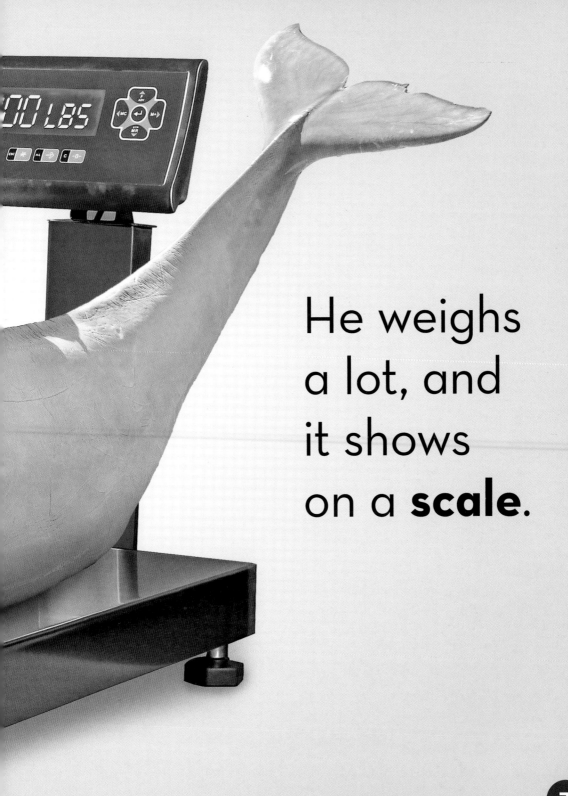

He weighs
a lot, and
it shows
on a **scale**.

He loves to eat fish but doesn't like **kale**.

Marco also loves squid but hates ginger **ale**.

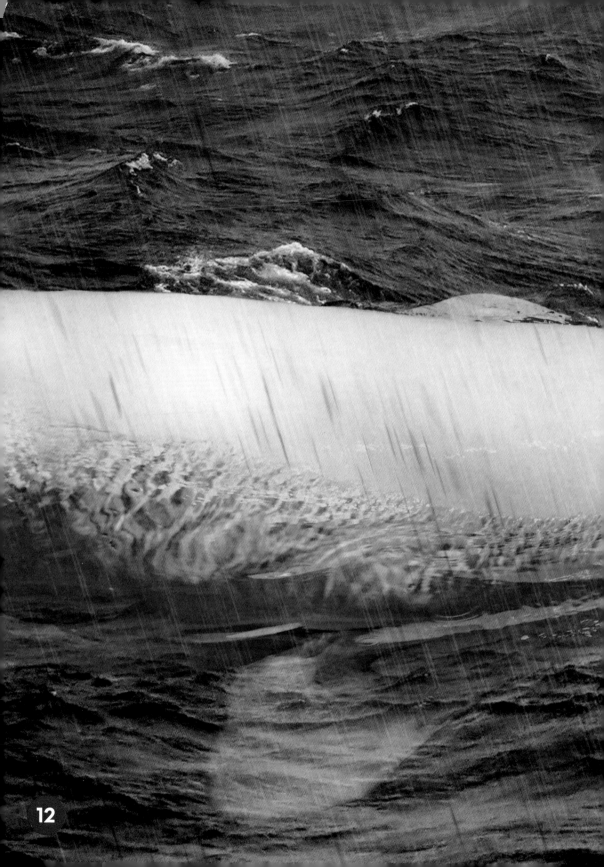

He breathes in air
even during a **gale**.

Marco is the star of his own **whale tale**!

Key Words in the -ale Family

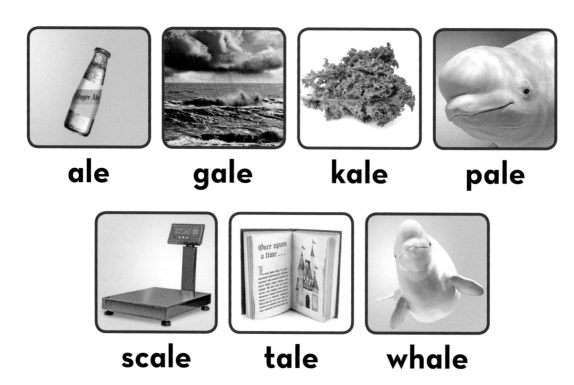

ale   gale   kale   pale

scale   tale   whale

Other **-ale** Words: **bale, male, sale**

Index

About the Author

Spencer Brinker loves to tell "dad jokes" and play word games with his twin girls.

Teaching Tips

Before Reading

✔ Introduce rhyming words and the **–ale** word family to readers.

✔ Guide readers on a "picture walk" through the text by asking them to name the things shown.

✔ Discuss book structure by showing children where text will appear consistently on pages. Highlight the supportive pattern of the book.

During Reading

✔ Encourage readers to "read with your finger" and point to each word as it is read. Stop periodically to ask children to point to a specific word in the text.

✔ Reading strategies: When encountering unknown words, prompt readers with encouraging cues such as:

- **Does that word look like a word you already know?**
- **Does it rhyme with another word you have already read?**

After Reading

✔ Write the key words on index cards.

- **Have readers match them to pictures in the book.**

✔ Ask readers to identify their favorite page in the book. Have them read that page aloud.

✔ Choose an **–ale** word. Ask children to pick a word that rhymes with it.

✔ Ask children to create their own rhymes using **–ale** words. Encourage them to use the same pattern found in the book.

Credits: Cover, © Miles Away Photography/Shutterstock; 2–3, © Luna Vandoorne/Shutterstock; 4–5, © CampCrazy Photography/Shutterstock and © Mansiliya Yury/Shutterstock; 6–7, © svrid79/Shutterstock and © tahir imran/Shutterstock; 8–9, © Daleen Loest/Shutterstock, © Mansiliya Yury/Shutterstock, and © Binh Thanh Bui/Shutterstock; 10–11, © Jiang Hongyan/Shutterstock, © Luna Vandoorne/Shutterstock, and © easy camera/Shutterstock; 12–13, © panparinda/Shutterstock and © Maksimilian/Shutterstock; 14–15, © Stask/iStock; 16T (L to R), © easy camera/Shutterstock, © Galyna Andrusko/Shutterstock, © Binh Thanh Bui/Shutterstock, and © CampCrazy Photography/Shutterstock; 16BL, © tahir imran/Shutterstock; 16BC, © Africa Studio/Shutterstock, © KateVogel/Shutterstock, and © Skorik Ekaterina/Shutterstock; 16BR, © racheldonahue/iStock.

Publisher: Kenn Goin   **Senior Editor:** Joyce Tavolacci   **Creative Director:** Spencer Brinker

Library of Congress Cataloging-in-Publication Data: Names: Brinker, Spencer, author. | Gambro, Beth, consultant. Title: A whale of a tale / by Spencer Brinker; consultant: Beth Gambro, Reading Specialist, Yorkville, Illinois. Description: New York, New York: Bearport Publishing, [2020] | Series: Read and rhyme: Level 3 | Includes index. Identifiers: LCCN 2019007345 (print) | LCCN 2019012635 (ebook) | ISBN 9781642806106 (Ebook) | ISBN 9781642805567 (library) | ISBN 9781642807257 (pbk.) Subjects: LCSH: Readers (Primary) | Whales—Juvenile fiction. Classification: LCC PE1119 (ebook) | LCC PE1119 .B751876 2020 (print) | DDC 428.6/2–dc23 LC record available at https://lccn.loc.gov/2019007345

Copyright © 2020 Bearport Publishing Company, Inc. All rights reserved. No part of this publication may be reproduced in whole or in part, stored in any retrieval system, or transmitted in any form or by any means, electronic, mechanical, photocopying, recording, or otherwise, without written permission from the publisher. For more information, write to Bearport Publishing Company, Inc., 45 West 21 Street, Suite 3B, New York, New York, 10010. Printed in the United States of America.

10 9 8 7 6 5 4 3 2 1